BOUNDARIES

How to Set Them— How to Keep Them

JUNE HUNT

Boundaries: How to Set Them—How to Keep Them
Copyright © 2018 Hope For The Heart
Aspire Press is an imprint of Rose Publishing, LLC.
P. O. Box 3473
Peabody, Massachusetts 01961-3473
www.hendricksonrose.com

For more information on Hope For The Heart, visit www.hopefortheheart.org or call 1-800-488-HOPE (4673).

Printed by Regent Publishing Services Ltd.
Printed in China
November 2017, 1st printing

CONTENTS

Dear Friend,

Boundaries—specifically how to establish and maintain healthy boundaries has been difficult for me. For some of us, relationship boundaries will be especially difficult if we grew up in a family where *boundaries* didn't exist or where they were skewed by dysfunctional behavior. I know this firsthand.

Let me tell you about "Deb" who had a heart to help our ministry . . . and me. Smart, competent, artistic, Deb was invaluable as a "can do" worker.

Despite wonderful qualities, however, Deb could be controlling. Given my propensity to be a *peace-at-any-price* person, I often allowed her to control *me*. (Notice my words: *I allowed her!*)

Sometimes Deb would speak harshly to me—even in front of others. Or, if Deb didn't agree with my wording in a magazine, she would insist that her changes be made (although I was head of the ministry).

Sometimes she made untrue accusations. No matter my explanation, she refused to accept the truth. I felt stymied and stuck. I hate to admit this, but sometimes I even confessed I was wrong when I knew I wasn't—just to get past the impasse. (Now, that's really wrong!)

Deb became increasingly disrespectful. Several people revealed negative comments she'd made about me. Some asked, "June, why do you let her talk to you this way? Why don't you stand up for yourself? You shouldn't let her control you." (They were right.)

How well I remember establishing my first boundary with Deb. I laid the groundwork with these words (her responses in parentheses):

"Do you want us to have the best relationship possible?" (*Yes.*)

"Do you believe we're truly encouraging each other?" (*No.*)

"In friendship, both should be better because of each other, like *iron sharpening iron*. Do you agree?" (*Yes, I do.*)

"Do you think we are both better?" (*No.*)

"Deb, I value our friendship, but when you explode in anger, it hurts both of us." (*I agree.*)

"So, in the future, if either of us expresses anger inappropriately, we need to step back and part ways for a while so that we don't damage our relationship further."

Deb said she understood, but the boundary hadn't been tested. However, that time came within a week.

While driving from my office to Deb's home, I began listening to my voicemail—then all of a sudden I heard her attacking, caustic voice, "Where are you? Where have you been? Why aren't you here?" She sounded out of control.

Four minutes later when I arrived at her house, Deb was calm and asked, "*Are you ready to go?*"

I hesitated. "Well, actually *no*. Remember our previous agreement about what would happen when one of us exploded in anger? We agreed to part ways for a time."

"*You can't leave!*" She exploded in an angry tirade that continued for several minutes.

Holding up my hand (palm toward her), I firmly said, "Stop!" To my astonishment, she did—she stopped!

Speaking in a slow, low voice I said, "Obviously now is not a good time for us to be together." Again, deliberately speaking slow and low, I said, "I'm going to leave."

Shocked, Deb said, "*You're already here! You can't leave.*"

I repeated our agreement: "If either of us expresses excessive anger, we agreed to not be together temporarily. So I need to leave. Later on, we can try again."

I drove away amid great protest. Deb kept calling my cell phone and home phone. (I didn't answer.) Candidly, I was amazed that I'd set a boundary and kept it!

Why this temporary separation? Because Proverbs 22:24 wisely advises: "*Do not make friends with a hot-tempered person, do not associate with one easily angered.*"

Two days later, she tearfully apologized, and for two weeks, no explosions occurred. However, the next time Deb vented, I left again—and perhaps eight more times over a twelve-month period—with much less intensity each time. Eventually, the outbursts ceased.

As I look back, Deb had respected me less and less. I would say, "You don't treat anyone else this way—why me?" She always answered, "I don't know."

The truth is, I *allowed* myself to be her verbal punching bag. But finally when I enforced the boundary, the verbal venom *decreased* and her respect for me *increased*. (I hadn't expected that.)

In reality, a relationship either "grows" or "goes." It *grows* mutually rewarding or it just *goes* astray, or maybe even *goes away*.

You can't make another person change. People have the choice to change, to be respectful—or not. Our responsibility is to enforce proper boundaries, which could challenge people to change. Just watch and see!

Hold on to hope,

June

June Hunt

P. S. God's Word exhorts us to "*show proper respect to everyone*" (1 Peter 2:17). Respect is at the heart of healthy boundaries. You'll be amazed at how many people will change—when you do your part.

BOUNDARIES

How to Set Them—How to Keep Them

Are you feeling stretched beyond your limits? Are you overcommitted, burning the candle at both ends? Are you trying to be everything to everyone? If so, *you* need boundaries!

Do people often take advantage of you? Do you say *yes* to everyone and *no* to no one? Do you think everyone's need is yours to meet? If so, you need *boundaries*!

You need to know where your responsibility ends and someone else's begins. At times, you need to say *no* to people so you can say yes to God.

Just as nations have protective boundaries, your relationships need protective boundaries to guard your personal time, emotional energy, and physical strength.

You cannot *be everything* or *do everything* for everyone—or even anyone. Therefore, you must choose how you relate to people in your life.

Notice how Jesus established a boundary in His relationship with two of His disciples. Brothers James and John said, "'*Let one of us sit at your right and the other at your left in your glory.*' . . . '*You don't know what you are asking,' Jesus said*" (Mark 10:37–38).

When the ten other disciples heard about their presumptive desire, they became angry. Then Jesus refuted their request with this contrast . . .

"Whoever wants to become great among you must be your servant, and whoever wants to be first must be slave of all." (Mark 10:43–44)

DEFINITIONS

Boundaries! They were vital when God brought forth something from nothing. One of the most vivid pictures of *physical boundaries* is recorded in the Bible when the Creator Himself poses a litany of rhetorical questions to the man named Job who is questioning the goodness of God.

Consider a few of these rapid-fire questions:

"Where were you when I laid the earth's foundation? . . . Who marked off its dimensions? . . . Who stretched a measuring line across it? . . . Who laid its cornerstone? Who shut up the sea behind doors . . . when I fixed limits for it . . . when I said, 'This far you may come and no farther; here is where your proud waves halt'?" (Job 38:2–4, 8, 10–11).

God directly confronts Job's wrong thinking, thus his heart becomes deeply humbled.

"I know that you can do all things;
no purpose of yours can be thwarted.
You asked, 'Who is this that obscures my plans without knowledge?'
Surely I spoke of things I did not understand,
things too wonderful for me to know. . . .
My ears had heard of you
but now my eyes have seen you.
Therefore I despise myself
and repent in dust and ashes."
(Job 42:2–3, 5–6)

Boundaries are such an indispensable part of daily life, they often exist unnoticed.

Physical boundaries say: "My body is mine—your body is yours." They keep us in our own lane and out of someone else's lane.

Personal boundaries say: "I am me, you are you. This is *my* responsibility—that is *yours*."

Spiritual boundaries keep our eyes on God's purpose for us and off His purpose for someone else. "God's plan for me is this. God's plan for you is *something else*."

God created boundaries by establishing fixed limits, but He Himself is limitless.

> **"Great is our Lord and mighty in power; his understanding has no limit."**
> **(Psalm 147:5)**

▶ Boundaries are established limits

- A marked limit of an area

  Example: *Sports*—Many sports have marked boundary lines defining the playing field (e.g., for football, baseball, soccer, tennis). All competition is confined to that designated area alone. When competitors step "out of bounds" or balls cross over the line, an immediate *repercussion* occurs (the action momentarily stops).

- A limit creating necessary space

  Example: *Relationships*—All healthy relationships have boundaries—*rewards* for right interactions and *repercussions* for wrong interactions. When someone becomes belittling, disrespectful, or destructive, this negative behavior creates the necessity for space between two people.

  Limiting the relationship is appropriate at destructive times (e.g., when someone becomes abusive, addicted, or expresses excessive anger).

  "A hot-tempered person must pay the penalty; rescue them, and you will have to do it again" (Proverbs 19:19).

▶ Boundaries are dividing lines

- A line separating one entity from another

  Example: *Territories*—Territorial borders are dividing lines (e.g., separating countries, states, counties, cities, even personal and business properties). The Niagara River divides Canada from the USA by forming the eastern boundary of both countries. To gain permission to go across the border of countries, people must possess passports. However, violators of passport or visa restrictions can receive the *repercussion* of being jailed or deported.

- A line not to be crossed

  Examples: *Laws*—Among civil law, drivers are not allowed to drive on sidewalks. A curb is a boundary. Because the boundary of a curb is the protective edge of a sidewalk, if drivers cross over the curb onto the sidewalk, they could experience numerous *repercussions* (e.g., killing a pedestrian, hitting stationary objects, receiving a fine).

Likewise, *biblical laws* are also lines not to be crossed. These laws (don't lie, don't steal, don't envy) benefit all people and show them how best to live with one another. Those who break biblical laws experience numerous *repercussions,* thus losing the blessing of God.

Deuteronomy 30:19 states, *"I have set before you life and death, blessings and curses. Now choose life, so that you and your children may live."*

Boundaries at the Beginning of Human History

- **Physical boundaries** are territorial lines that divide one area from another.

  - Anyone who owns a piece of property has the *right to control* that property and the *responsibility to set rules* for people on the property. In the Bible, the first boundary given to a person was spoken directly from God to Adam.

    "You are free to eat from any tree in the garden, but you must not eat from the tree of the knowledge of good and evil'" (Genesis 2:16–17).

  - You have the right of personal control over what is yours and the responsibility of setting rules for others regarding what is yours. As creator and owner of the Garden of Eden, God had the right to set rules for everything and everyone in the garden.

"For when you eat from it [the tree] you will certainly die."' (Genesis 2:17).

- **Moral boundaries** are ethical lines that divide right from wrong.

  - When a *boundary is respected*, the result is a *reward.* God set a moral boundary for Adam and Eve—based on right and wrong. When the boundary was honored, the couple enjoyed a reward—the abundance of the garden and unbroken fellowship with God.

    When a *boundary is rejected*, the result is a *repercussion.* When God's boundary was violated, the couple experienced a *repercussion*—sin entered the world, which disqualified Adam and Eve from staying within the bounds of the garden.

  - When you communicate a clear, rightful boundary—with a *reward* and a *repercussion*—yet someone violates that boundary, the repercussion is to be inevitable, and if possible, instantaneous. In choosing to violate a boundary, *the violator*, not you, *is choosing the repercussion.*

    The principle of *rewards* and *repercussions* was clearly demonstrated when God set a boundary with Adam. By choosing to violate the boundary established by the Lord, *he chose the repercussion* assigned to their sin.

    "Because you listened to your wife and ate fruit from the tree about which I commanded you, "You must not eat from it," Cursed is the ground because of you; through painful toil you will eat food from it all the days of your life' " (Genesis 3:17).

- **Personal boundaries** are lines that separate one person from another.
  - *Personal boundaries* are the healthy by-product of realizing we are uniquely separate from one another and personally responsible for our own responses. Adam and Eve clearly knew God's rule with the repercussion, yet the Serpent (Satan) spoke to Eve, "*You will not certainly die . . . you will be like God*" (Genesis 3:4–5).
    - Eve lacked *personal boundaries*—she allowed the serpent to have undue influence over her.
    - Adam lacked *personal boundaries*—he allowed Eve to have undue influence over him.

  However, after God confronted them about eating the forbidden fruit, Adam blamed Eve, and then Eve blamed the Serpent. Neither took personal responsibility for violating the boundary.

  " '*The woman you put here with me—she gave me some fruit from the tree, and I ate it.' . . . The woman said, 'The serpent deceived me, and I ate'* " (Genesis 3:12–13).

  - *Personal boundaries* mean you alone are responsible for your own choices. Boundaries are integral to your individual identity (who you uniquely are) as well as your individual decisions and responsibilities. Adam and Eve needed to think as *individuals* about what God said regardless of what others said. For to not stay within God's boundary caused a repercussion that changed their lives—and ours—forever.

  "*The Lord God banished him [and her] from the Garden of Eden*" (Genesis 3:23 NLT).

WHAT IS the Purpose of Personal Boundaries?

Personal boundaries are powerful protectors. The boundary of a tiger's cage keeps a dangerous tiger *inside* the cage and keeps vulnerable people *outside* the cage. In relationships, boundaries are put in place to guard, to protect, and to provide a healthy environment for relationships to flourish and grow toward Christlike maturity.

Have you ever experienced the pain of someone hurting you?

You shouldn't be surprised. The Bible says, "*The heart is devious above all else?*" (Jeremiah 17:9 NRSV).

Therefore, boundaries are necessary to protect you from devious attackers. The Bible reveals the treasure within you that is to be guarded above everything else.

"Above all else, guard your heart,
for everything you do flows from it."
(Proverbs 4:23)

▶ **Personal boundaries allow you to:**

- **Determine** what belongs to you and what belongs to another
- **Decide** who and what you will prioritize in your life
- **Demonstrate** how you will maintain control over your body, soul, and spirit
- **Declare** limits in your relationships—and your right to enforce them
- **Designate** your unique gifts and assignments that align with your calling
- **Delineate** how you will maintain your moral convictions, not violating your conscience

Have you been pressured to do something that brought chaos into your life?

Personal boundaries bring order to your life. The Bible says . . .

> **"Everything should be done in a fitting and orderly way."**
> **(1 Corinthians 14:40)**

▶ **Personal boundaries convey:**

- What you are *and* what you aren't
- What you value *and* what you don't
- What you believe *and* what you don't
- What you'll endure *and* what you won't
- What you'll accept *and* what you won't
- What you'll give *and* what you won't

Have you been manipulated to give money and later regretted it?

Pray for wisdom to establish the best boundaries possible. They will help you be the best person possible, have the healthiest relationships possible, and make the best decisions possible.

"How much better to get wisdom than gold, to get insight rather than silver!" (Proverbs 16:16)

WHAT ARE the Benefits of Personal Boundaries?

Imagine a fence around your home. That fence protects young children from wandering into the street—perhaps from being injured, kidnapped, or even killed. Likewise, fences also provide barriers against strangers and keep strays from entering your property.

Personal boundaries are like fences—protecting you from wrong people, wrong places, and wrong priorities. Personal boundaries also guard you from giving more time, talent, and tolerance than you should—protecting you from people taking more than they should. Boundaries also make it possible for you to enjoy mutual give-and-take within healthy relationships.

Have you been repeatedly taken advantage of by a "taker"?

In life, there are *givers* and *takers*. Instead of believing everything you're told, biblical wisdom warns you to be prudent and not taken in.

"The simple believe anything, but the prudent give thought to their steps." (Proverbs 14:15)

▶ **Relational boundaries enable you to:**

- **Stand up** for yourself, speak your mind, and share your relationship restrictions appropriately
- **Feel** comfortable giving honest feedback without fear
- **Be firm** with others in a thoughtful and unapologetic way
- **Respect** the rules of others and act in their best interest
- **Establish** and maintain healthy give-and-take relationships
- **Defend** others and promote equality in your relationships

Have you had a "one-sided" relationship in which you don't feel valued?

Jesus establishes your foundation for healthy relationships—live by The Golden Rule.

"Do to others as you would have them do to you." (Luke 6:31)

▶ Emotional and mental boundaries equip you to:

- **Evaluate** the appropriateness of your thoughts and emotions in light of God's Word
- **Guard** against letting your own emotions—or someone else's—control you
- **Investigate** truth for yourself and to keep decisions governed by God
- **Feel** the freedom to agree or disagree with others without fear or guilt
- **Communicate** your own thoughts and emotions in a Christlike way
- **Disengage** from those who try to manipulate, hurt, or lie to you

Have you been mentally shot down, causing you to feel emotionally shut down?

The Bible communicates how to deal with lies and deception and how to live in the light of truth.

"We demolish arguments and every pretension that sets itself up against the knowledge of God, and we take captive every thought to make it obedient to Christ." (2 Corinthians 10:5)

▶ Spiritual boundaries allow you to:

- **Enjoy** a right relationship with God by entrusting your life to Christ
- **Distinguish** God's will for you as opposed to the will of others imposed on you

- **Commit** to being controlled by Christ, not controlled by others
- **Avoid** spiritually divisive people and enjoy healthy, encouraging Christians
- **Refuse** being manipulated by spiritual leaders and those who twist Scripture
- **Live** in a way that first pleases God, not living as a people pleaser

Have you felt pressured to please people—instead of pleasing God?

The Bible presents these challenging questions.

> **"Am I now trying to win the approval of human beings, or of God? Or am I trying to please people? If I were still trying to please people, I would not be a servant of Christ."**
> **(Galatians 1:10)**

▶ **Moral and ethical boundaries teach you to:**

- **Know** the difference between right and wrong
- **Discern** the true character of a person
- **Act** on the courage of your convictions
- **Say** *no* to people so you can say *yes* to God
- **Live** a life of integrity, being the same in the dark as you are in the light
- **Evaluate** the right way to think, feel, and act toward others

Have you been required to violate your conscience or lie because of imposed loyalty?

The Lord requires you to do only what is right.

"The Lord has told you what is good,
and this is what he requires of you:
to do what is right,
to love mercy,
and to walk humbly with your God."
(Micah 6:8 NLT)

► **Sexual boundaries empower you to:**

- **Define** your areas of appropriate sexual expression
- **Discern** what of a sexual nature you will not allow yourself to watch, hear, and participate in
- **Determine** whether or not you will allow yourself to be sexually touched, verbally seduced, or emotionally enticed
- **Decide** the parameters you will place on your thought life regarding sex
- **Delay** sexual activity for a committed marriage relationship
- **Detail** how you will respond in the heat of passionate temptation

Have you struggled with sexual boundaries—not knowing how to hold the line?

God's Word clearly states these sexual boundaries are not to be violated.

"It is God's will that you should be sanctified:
that you should avoid sexual immorality;
that each of you should learn
to control your own body
in a way that is holy and honorable."
(1 Thessalonians 4:3–4)

▶ **Physical boundaries help you to:**

- **Guard** yourself against abusive people
- **Maintain** a sense of being separate and uniquely you
- **Prevent** physical injury to yourself and to others
- **Protect** your personal individuality when with others
- **Avoid** the appearance of impropriety
- **Explore** your own individual interests, strengths, aptitudes, and desires

Have you been manipulated with words like "You must do this with me. You owe me."?

God's Word says your body belongs to God.

"Do you not know that your body is the
temple of the Holy Spirit who is in you,
whom you have from God,
and you are not your own?
For you were bought at a price;
therefore glorify God in your body."
(1 Corinthians 6:19–20 NKJV)

Healthy Boundaries

Question: "What role do boundaries play in relationships, and how important is it to establish boundaries?"

Answer: People with healthy boundaries understand (1) our unique *individuality* and (2) our need for separateness, which is mutually beneficial. While we are separate from one another, God created us to be in relationship with one another. The way we succeed at being both separate and together is accomplished through healthy boundaries.

Healthy people have healthy relationships because they understand what healthy boundaries provide:

- Security and confidence in who we are as individual creations of God
- The ability to say *yes* and *no* to others without guilt or fear
- Fences that keep us not from loving each other—but from harming each other.

With boundaries, we are able to juggle togetherness and separateness by creating and maintaining balance in our relationships. We do this by giving God His proper place and people their proper place. When God comes first and people come second, we have godly *companionship* with one another.

"Jesus replied: 'Love the Lord your God with all your heart and with all your soul and with all your mind.' This is the first and greatest commandment. And the second is like it: 'Love your neighbor as yourself'" (Matthew 22:37–39).

WHAT IS God's Heart on Boundaries?

God created us to be His "image bearers"—literally to bear the image of God. In the first chapter of Genesis, God says, *"Let us make human beings in our image"* (Genesis 1:26 NLT). We are to be like Him in our character and to act like Him in our lives.

God's heart is that we set boundaries that are mutually beneficial for our relationships with one another, and He clearly communicates those boundaries in His Word. He gives us written boundaries to show us who He is and what He requires of us.

"Live in harmony with one another. Do not be proud. . . . Do not be conceited." (Romans 12:16)

God's Blueprint for Boundaried Relationships

God has ordained boundaries for us—boundaries we need to set and enforce. By understanding God's heart on boundaries, we can develop meaningful relationships that are pleasing to God and fulfilling to us. When this occurs ...

▶ We treat one another with respect.

"Show proper respect to everyone" (1 Peter 2:17).

▶ We listen to one another, considering our words before we speak.

"Everyone should be quick to listen, slow to speak" (James 1:19).

- We do not lie, but rather speak truthfully to one another from our hearts.

  "Each of you must put off falsehood and speak truthfully to your neighbor" (Ephesians 4:25).

- We say *yes* or *no* without lengthy justification or feeling guilty.

  "All you need to say is simply 'Yes' or 'No'" (Matthew 5:37).

- We give and accept correction while refraining from flattery.

  "Whoever rebukes a person will in the end gain favor rather than one who has a flattering tongue" (Proverbs 28:23).

- We confront one another if we sin against one other.

  "If your brother or sister sins, go and point out their fault, just between the two of you. If they listen to you, you have won them over" (Matthew 18:15).

- We express anger in a helpful, not hurtful, manner.

  "In your anger do not sin" (Ephesians 4:26).

- We take responsibility for our wrongs and forgive when we've been wronged.

  "Be kind and compassionate to one another, forgiving each other, just as in Christ God forgave you" (Ephesians 4:32).

- We encourage one another—verbally, emotionally, and spiritually.

  "Let us not neglect our meeting together . . . but encourage one another" (Hebrews 10:25 NLT).

- ▶ We practice mutual submission.

  "Submit to one another out of reverence for Christ" (Ephesians 5:21).

- ▶ We remove ourselves from abusive situations.

  "Do not make friends with a hot-tempered person, do not associate with one easily angered" (Proverbs 22:24).

- ▶ We refuse to stay in a relationship if either of us is negatively influenced.

  "Do not be misled: 'Bad company corrupts good character'" (1 Corinthians 15:33).

Following God's blueprint for boundaries, we build strong relationships as well as godly character.

CHARACTERISTICS

After his wife dies, 81-year-old Larry continues living at home, but he needs regular assistance with shopping for groceries, supplies, and other chores. His daughter Loretta, a nurse, drives an hour on Saturdays to help. However, a problem soon arises over Larry's coarse language. Like fingernails on a chalkboard, his language becomes so grating that Loretta realizes she must set a boundary.

"Dad, I love you and always want to help you. But your coarse language is offensive to me. It wounds my spirit. You can choose to continue to speak this way, but if you do, that will let me know you don't want my help, and I'll leave. But understand, *you'll be choosing* to be without my help."

The next week when Loretta arrives to tackle Dad's to-do list, the profanity starts within 15 minutes. "Dad, I was willing to help you but since you've chosen to continue using offensive language, I told you I would leave. Obviously, you don't want my help now."

"What? You can't leave! You promised to help!" Larry yells.

"I want to help, but this is *your* choice. I'll be back next week, and we'll try again."

Loretta leaves hurt. Her dad is hurt, but he chose to cross the line—the boundary line of inappropriateness. So she follows through with the repercussion. She also returns the following week. Her father greets her and remains a perfect gentleman during that Saturday and the next . . . and the next. However, during the fourth visit, he tests her resolve with more coarse language.

"Oh, Dad. I'm so sorry you don't want my help this week. I love you, and I'll see you next week." And off she trots. That does it! It only takes a few more times of testing, and within a few months, her father treats her with new value and a new vocabulary. These boundaries are not about winning a game. For this dad/daughter duo, it's about winning a relationship—a new relationship of respect. Proverbs 12:18 paints this picture . . .

"The words of the reckless pierce like swords, but the tongue of the wise brings healing."

WHAT Distinguishes Bad Boundaries from Beneficial Boundaries?

Beneficial boundaries are loving and are aimed at honoring, respecting, and protecting ourselves and others. Those looking for a litmus test for evaluating beneficial boundaries need to look closely at 1 Corinthians 13:4–8, where love is described:

> *"Love is patient, love is kind. It does not envy, it does not boast, it is not proud. It does not dishonor others, it is not self-seeking, it is not easily angered, it keeps no record of wrongs. Love does not delight in evil but rejoices with the truth. It always protects, always trusts, always hopes, always perseveres. Love never fails."*

As you distinguish bad boundaries from beneficial boundaries, be aware of the following differences in progression between these two types of boundary setters.

Bad Boundaries vs. Beneficial Boundaries

True Scenario: Someone intentionally misrepresented the truth about your words. It's called slander. You're upset. You know the rumor mill will further distort the truth unless you take action to stop it. What you do next will determine whether you practice bad or beneficial boundaries.

If You Have Bad Boundaries . . .	If You Have Beneficial Boundaries . . .
You have enmeshed relationships but no true intimacy. You retreat within yourself, concealing your inner most feelings. You feel unsafe confronting, so you keep your guard up, believing no one genuinely cares for you.	You have many acquaintances but choose to be totally open and truly transparent with only the few who have proven themselves safe—those who have your best interest at heart.
"A friend loves at all times, and a brother is born for a time of adversity." (Proverbs 17:17)	

If You Have Bad Boundaries . . .	If You Have Beneficial Boundaries . . .
When finally confronting the offender, you become inconsistent, stumbling, and rigid. When challenged, you overreact and over explain.	When confronting the offender, you are consistent and calm, respectful and firm, straightforward and assertive. When challenged, you stay centered and succinct.
"All you need to say is simply 'Yes' or 'No'." (Matthew 5:37).	
You don't enforce the repercussion for negative behavior. Therefore, the offender—known for untrustworthy character—stays in your life only to cause more painful consequences. You are misled, thinking this slanderer won't do it again.	You enforce repercussions onto the slanderer for the unacceptable behavior. If no change occurs, you act to discontinue the relationship. You reward positive change of behavior with encouraging compliments to help the relationship flourish.
"Do not be misled: 'Bad company corrupts good character'." (1 Corinthians 15:33).	

<table>
<tr><th>If You Have Bad Boundaries . . .</th><th>If You Have Beneficial Boundaries . . .</th></tr>
<tr><td>You're afraid to confront because you fear people won't agree with you. This leaves you feeling inferior.</td><td>You're not afraid to confront respectfully, because you trust the Lord is leading you to do what is right.</td></tr>
<tr><td colspan="2">"Fear of man will prove to be a snare, but whoever trusts in the Lord is kept safe." (Proverbs 29:25)</td></tr>
<tr><td>You isolate yourself in order to minimize exposure to the offender, and you see yourself as a victim. You don't ask for what needs to change.</td><td>Even at the risk of being hurt, you form a relationship based on respectful communication in order to ask for change from the offender.</td></tr>
<tr><td colspan="2">"You do not have because you do not ask God." (James 4:2)</td></tr>
<tr><td>You define yourself based on what others say or feel about you, and you'll do almost anything to feel accepted by them.</td><td>You define yourself based on what God says about you. You know you are accepted by God, so you aren't controlled by others.</td></tr>
<tr><td colspan="2">"Accept one another, then, just as Christ accepted you, in order to bring praise to God." (Romans 15:7)</td></tr>
</table>

If You Have Bad Boundaries . . .	If You Have Beneficial Boundaries . . .
You cannot understand how the offender could wrong you, thus you come to a false conclusion. Self-deceived, you simply say, "I can't do anything about it."	You identify how the offender has chosen wrong and confront, stating the boundary. Then you state the repercussion if the offense is repeated.
"The wisdom of the prudent is to give thought to their ways, but the folly of fools is deception." (Proverbs 14:8)	
You use emotional manipulation to attack indirectly—by assigning negative motives. You view disagreeing with someone as aggression and don't want to incite anger.	You express the facts, how you feel, and what you want in a forthright way. You maintain dialogue in a spirit of openness and discovery.
"The tongue has the power of life and death." (Proverbs 18:21)	

If You Have Bad Boundaries . . .	If You Have Beneficial Boundaries . . .
You use boundaries as a weapon against others, to exert power over them. You deceive them through lies and half-truths, and to keep them off balance and at a distance.	You use boundaries as an accurate safeguard, demonstrating your desire to maintain a healthy, honest, God-honoring relationship.
"Do not lie to each other, since you have taken off your old self with its practices." (Colossians 3:9)	
You don't communicate anything of depth because you have difficulty trusting people. You don't rely on anyone for counsel.	Although not everyone is trustworthy, you do have a few trustworthy friends. You can rely on their counsel.
"One who has unreliable friends soon comes to ruin, but there is a friend who sticks closer than a brother." (Proverbs 18:24)	

WHAT Is a Checklist for Boundaryless People?

As you think about the many times you've lacked boundaries, place a check mark (✔) in the box beside the following statements that are generally true of you:

Checklist for the Boundaryless

- ❏ I have difficulty making decisions and sticking with them if someone opposes them.
- ❏ I feel like I must seek the opinions of others before acting on a decision.
- ❏ I fear expressing what I really feel.
- ❏ I lack confidence in my own convictions.
- ❏ I avoid certain people because I fear I might be embarrassed.
- ❏ I have difficulty maintaining eye contact with others.
- ❏ I am reluctant to ask others for help.
- ❏ I dread losing the love and affection of others.
- ❏ I perform favors for others even when I know I shouldn't.
- ❏ I avoid asking people to return overdue items they've borrowed.
- ❏ I need a great deal of assurance from others.
- ❏ I allow others to be untruthful by failing to correct them.

- ❑ I have difficulty pointing out unfair situations.
- ❑ I say *yes* when I want to say *no*.
- ❑ I think I have to answer the phone every time it rings.
- ❑ I typically listen to a telemarketer even when I want to say, "No, thank you."
- ❑ I feel compelled to send money when I receive solicitations or requests for donations.
- ❑ I feel guilty when I say no to someone who is asking for my time.
- ❑ I sometimes accept the blame for the mistakes of others.
- ❑ I feel guilty when someone suffers a repercussion for breaking a boundary I set.

If you struggle with broken boundaries, you may have excessive fear of disappointing others, receiving criticism, or losing love. The Lord doesn't want you to live in a state of fear but rather in the confident assurance of His constant presence.

For the next three weeks, read the following verses out loud every day to reinforce that He is your strength, He is your confidence, and He is your security.

"The Lord is my light and my salvation—whom shall I fear? The Lord is the stronghold of my life—of whom shall I be afraid? . . . Though an army besiege me, my heart will not fear; though war break out against me, even then I will be confident."
(Psalm 27:1, 3)

WHAT Characterizes People Whose Boundaries Are Violated?

People who grow up with few or no boundaries become accustomed to having their own rights violated. Mistreatment is mainstream. In their frustration or attempt at self-preservation, many perpetuate the pattern by mistreating others themselves, often without understanding what they are doing or why. They simply live out what they have learned through their own personal experience—"You do unto others what was done to you!" Or they model the more passive responses of other abuse victims.

Letting go of the victim mentality is not easy, however, the Bible says . . .

"It is for freedom that Christ has set us free. Stand firm, then, and do not let yourselves be burdened again by a yoke of slavery."
(Galatians 5:1)

Signs of Crossed Boundaries

Those who are boundaryless tend to develop the following shared characteristics:

- **Non-confrontational**—Skills necessary for confronting problem people are virtually nonexistent or ineffective. Rather than dealing directly with those needing boundaries, they either become emotionally, verbally, or physically abusive, or they simply fail to set appropriate limits—lack of confrontation is blamed on others.

- **Irresponsible**—Denial, justification, blame games, guilt trips, and other forms of manipulation replace the practice of assuming responsibility for their own inappropriate boundaries.
- **Closed**—Lack of openness, honesty, and transparency are typical. Skills for developing intimacy are considered foolish and unnecessary or even threatening and terrifying.
- **Secretive**—Following severe abuse, concealment is common, and even considered necessary for self-defense and self-preservation. Hiding the truth is especially prevalent in cases where sexual boundaries have been violated.
- **Inconsistent**—Strategies for implementing repercussions and rewards are virtually nonexistent. Inconsistency reigns in every area, resulting in continued confusion and distrust.
- **Envious**—With a sense of inadequacy and insecurity, continual striving for approval, attention, affirmation, and acceptance feels necessary. When another person's performance excels, envy can be the natural by-product.
- **Defensive**—Self-preserving behaviors reflect a need to deny feelings of being unloved, insignificant, and insecure. Feeling defensive about unhealthy relationships, adult daughters often want to remain "daddy's little princess" and grown sons want to be "mommy's little prince" rather than becoming emotionally invested in healthy relationships.

Recognizing that personal boundaries have been repeatedly violated and then working through the pain of that awareness to make necessary changes takes courage, tenacity, and hope.

God not only meets our needs but gives us far more than we could ever ask or imagine. When we are rooted in the security of God's love, we find . . .

> **"I pray that you, being rooted and established in love, may have power, together with all the Lord's holy people, to grasp how wide and long and high and deep is the love of Christ, and to know this love that surpasses knowledge— that you may be filled to the measure of all the fullness of God."**
> **(Ephesians 3:17–19)**

WHAT Connects Codependency to Boundaries?

Codependency and a lack of boundaries go hand in hand. When you are in a codependent relationship, you depend on another person to the point of being addicted to that person, as well as open yourself up to being controlled and manipulated by them. Codependency is the natural by-product of having few or no boundaries because it is driven by the lack of personal wholeness and sufficiency.

The problem for those who are codependent is not their dependency but rather the *object* of their dependency. The fact is, we are all dependent, but our desire and focus should be on our Lord—our only true Need-Meeter—and not on another person. As the psalmist wrote regarding His relationship with God . . .

"I am always with you;
you hold me by my right hand.
You guide me with your counsel,
and afterward you will take me into glory.
Whom have I in heaven but you?
And earth has nothing I desire besides you.
My flesh and my heart may fail,
but God is the strength of my heart
and my portion forever."
(Psalm 73:23–26)

Codependency is . . .

- **Marked by** an insecure, dependent person spending an inordinate amount of time and energy meeting other people's needs and desires while neglecting their own personal needs and desires.
- **Based on** the belief that this subservient helper/rescuer has no real inherent value unless immersed in meeting others' needs as the enabler.
- **Rooted in** the premise that one person not only determines the worth of another person, but also has the power to control that person's thoughts, feelings, and circumstances.
- **Identified as** a relationship dominated by fear and control where power is exaggerated, misdirected, and generally abused.
- **Established by** boundary violators who manipulate to get their own way without regard for anyone else's feelings or desires.

- **Characterized by** unsolicited advice, deception, and intimidation as well as excessive control, anger, and intrusion.

Almost without fail, those who allow themselves to be held captive in codependent relationships find that . . .

"They loved human praise more than praise from God." (John 12:43)

WHAT Repercussions Result from Breaking Boundaries?

Boundaries typically come with rewards and repercussions—consequences that impart memorable lessons to willing learners. Stay within the boundaries, and there are rewards. Step outside the boundaries, and you receive repercussions. At times, we need to set specific boundaries and determine appropriate rewards and repercussions.

For example, if a friend routinely asks for a ride, but never offers to chip in for gas, you should set a boundary: "Pat, I don't mind giving you a ride when you truly need one, but it would help me out if we could split the cost of the gas. That way there is mutual give and take. I always want to show respect toward each other—and I would really feel respected with this arrangement. Is this agreeable with you?" (Wait for a response.) If no agreement is offered, "Then I think it would be best if you could make other arrangements."

The laws God established for the nation of Israel certainly reflect this premise . . .

"I wish their hearts would always respect me and that they would always obey my commands so that things would go well for them and their children forever!" (Deuteronomy 5:29 NCV)

Examples of broken boundaries and resulting repercussions include:

▶ **Money misused by a teenager.**

The money is reimbursed and further funds withheld until the responsible use of money is reestablished.

▶ **Lies told.**

Trust is withheld and verification of future information is required until the offender proves that truthfulness has become a priority.

▶ **Adultery committed.**

Contact with the third party stops, marriage and individual counseling starts, sexual relations between the marriage partners is suspended until receiving results of STD tests and suggested medical treatment is completed. Then faithfulness must be reestablished and trust rebuilt.

▶ **Abusive language.**

Interaction stops and time apart must be taken by both parties until civility in conversations is reestablished.

- **Inappropriate anger.**

  Causes for loss of control are explored and resolved through counseling. Anger management must be learned and demonstrated over time.

- **"No" ignored by a child.**

  The topic in question is temporarily off limits for discussion, and time-outs are enforced if resistance to being told *no* persists.

- **Time disrespected by a friend.**

  Meeting together is rescheduled after waiting a reasonable amount of time previously agreed on (e.g., 20 to 40 minutes). Separate modes of transportation are to be used if traveling together results in arriving late. Departures are scheduled so time won't be a factor.

When establishing repercussions, they must be clearly stated, realizing the goal of repercussions is not punishment but repentance and ultimate transformation.

Resistance toward a particular boundary indicates there is a problem that needs to be addressed, a hurt that needs to be healed, or a pattern of behavior that needs to be changed—for the good of the relationship and for mutual growth.

**"As iron sharpens iron,
so one person sharpens another."
(Proverbs 27:17)**

CAUSES

Roger and Susan consider themselves good parents. They take their two boys to church and actively support their efforts in school, sports, and scouting. They cheer their accomplishments and facilitate their education—all to help them succeed in life.

Yet, the parents' comfortable "nest" must seem difficult to leave—for now their "baby birds" are in their 30s—showing no signs of trying out their wings.

Both parents say they want their "boys" to be on their own, and their sons say they'd like to move out but just can't afford it. Of course, they'd have to leave the comfy all-bills-paid home plus TV, Internet, insurance, and other amenities.

Candidly, living on their own doesn't appeal to them. And why should it? They have all the comforts of home with little responsibility. When parents provide virtually everything for their capable adult children, they hinder their growth and maturity. If only Roger and Susan had implemented positive boundaries designed to encourage their boys to become motivated men, independent and strong—not unmotivated sons dependent on their parents.

God gives parents a fascinating picture, seen in nature, of urging offspring out of the "nest." Look at the life of the majestic eagle. Once hatched, the baby birds are completely dependent on their parent to feed them, keep them warm, and protect them. But when the time comes for their young to leave the nest, the large eagle demonstrates how to flap its wings, and then stirs the nest, removing feathers, leaves, and straw—all the soft linings.

Making the nest intentionally uncomfortable is one way to urge eaglets out of the nest and launch them into the sky. Yet, when eaglets first take flight, the parents watch in case the fledglings flounder. The protective parents stay ready to swoop in and carry the young bird back to the nest for another flying lesson until the young birds are soaring the skies all on their own.

The Old Testament paints this picture of the eagle doing its parenting job perfectly . . .

> **"Like an eagle that stirs up its nest**
> **and hovers over its young,**
> **that spreads its wings to catch them**
> **and carries them aloft."**
> **(Deuteronomy 32:11)**

WHAT Experiences Help Us Learn Boundaries?

Responsibilities assigned to us in life increase over time as we pass through various developmental stages. As toddlers, we learn to brush our teeth, bathe our bodies, and go to bed. Yet the fixed time we are to "be in bed" changes as we grow older. That's when "bedtime battles" over boundaries occur—especially through the teenage years.

Our lives are initially protected by parents (or other caregivers). They are the primary shapers of our childhood boundaries that become modified throughout our lives. These boundaries can be strong, effective, and helpful—or they can be weak, ineffective, and harmful.

Regardless of boundaries learned—or not learned—from the past, we have a perfect parent in our heavenly Father. He will teach us not to repeat past bad patterns and train us to experience new, positive patterns.

**"Forget the former things;
do not dwell on the past.
See, I am doing a new thing!"
(Isaiah 43:18–19)**

- **We learn boundaries** as we observe and experience the natural laws of God's created world.
- **We learn boundaries** from parents and other authorities who model boundaries as they teach, encourage, and correct in love.[1]
- **We learn boundaries** in our relationships with family, friends, and others.
- **We learn boundaries** as we grasp God's expectation that we reflect His character.
- **We learn boundaries** from making mistakes, from trial and error, and from painful consequences of our own bad choices.
- **We learn boundaries** by gaining wisdom from our own interactions and then by applying what really works.

The apostle Paul said …

"Join together in following my example, brothers and sisters, and just as you have us as a model, keep your eyes on those who live as we do." (Philippians 3:17)

WHAT IS the Process of Learning Boundaries As a Child?

By God's design, children are to be instructed by and learn boundaries from loving parents who have personally established healthy boundaries. Sadly, not all parents are committed to God's plan.

If parents never establish beneficial personal boundaries, how can they teach their children the importance of beneficial boundaries? The development of children follows a predictable course based on the type of parenting they receive. This is why the Bible emphasizes the importance of wise parenting.

"Listen, my son, to your father's instruction and do not forsake your mother's teaching." (Proverbs 1:8)

▶ As a parent responds to an infant's cries, the baby begins to:[2]

- Learn that someone is available to meet needs
- Enjoy a sense of having value and worth
- Find security in bonding relationships

- As the sense of security increases, the child begins to:[3]
    - Separate minimally from parents for small increments of time
    - Establish limited personal autonomy
    - Experience the exhilaration of exploration
- As feelings of security grow, the child begins to:[4]
    - Move back and forth between the secure parental relationships and the challenge of separation
    - Feel increased excitement and confidence to explore
    - Lay the foundation for formulating legitimate boundaries

In childhood, when the God-given needs for love, significance, and security aren't met, healthy independence isn't developed, which lays the foundation for future codependent relationships.[5] When we experience rejection rather than unconditional love, our "love bucket" (our internal capacity for love, significance, security, and acceptance) begins to leak and cannot be filled until those "holes"—or wounds—are healed.

Only the love of our perfect heavenly parent, God Himself, can reach deep enough to bring about complete healing.

"He heals the brokenhearted and binds up their wounds." (Psalm 147:3)

Boundaries for Kids

QUESTION: "How can I explain to my child the need for boundaries?"[6]

ANSWER: Over the years, I've shared this story *with all* ages—with great results:

Imagine a clever young goldfish gurgling, "I want to be free of this *fishbowl!* I don't like the boundary of this bowl! It's keeping me from going where I want to go and doing what I want to do—it's too limiting!"

So, one day the goldfish jumps a little here and leaps a little there. Finally, with the flip of his fins and a flap of his tail, he leaps outside the bowl.

The fish is free—clear of the fishbowl's boundary!

But what happens to our goldfish? In minutes, he dies. This one act dooms him to certain death. Why?

1. Goldfish need water.
2. The fishbowl held the needed water.
3. The boundary of the fishbowl held the water the goldfish needed for life.

Being free to do whatever you want may *seem* right, but that doesn't make it right. Proverbs 14:12 says, *"There is a way that appears to be right, but in the end it leads to death."* God gave you to me . . . and me to you. Part of my job is helping you *stay in the bowl* God has given you. As you grow, God has designed your bowl to grow right along with you, so it will always be just the right size!

WHAT ARE Five Biblical Truths about Boundaries?

Rhonda yearns to restore safety and sanity following the divorce from her physically abusive husband. Meanwhile 22-year-old Jared lives at home while finishing college. Previously abused by his father, he is now being verbally abusive toward his mother—plus shirking all responsibility.

When Rhonda insists he be respectful and responsible, he heaps on even more verbal abuse. With the help of church elders, Rhonda sets the boundary that he must be respectful or move out of her home. Instead, he becomes incensed—even to the point of filing a lawsuit against his own mother!

The court rules in her favor, and Jared is forced to move out—in two weeks. After she helps gather boxes and pack his car, he attacks her faith: "I can't believe you call yourself a Christian. You'll never see me graduate from law school. God would never evict His own son!"

Hesitantly, Rhonda reminds him, "Well, God did 'evict' Adam from the Garden."

"So the Lord God banished him from the Garden of Eden."
(Genesis 3:23)

And, yes, he floorboarded the car. And yes, after three years, he did call her to attend graduation. And yes, a respectful relationship has been restored—the proof of beneficial boundaries.

When God gave the first couple, Adam and Eve, a boundary about what they could and could not eat, they were initially compliant because they knew the Boundary-Giver to be loving, generous, and completely trustworthy. It wasn't until Satan created doubt about God's character that each chose to disobey God.

Had they not considered the possibility of God's withholding good from them, they would have remained respectfully and happily obedient to Him.

Sin thrives in the world today and clouds the perspective of many regarding boundaries. Like everything good God has put into place in His creation, boundaries have been maligned and misrepresented as being unloving and undesirable. But this is not true. Boundaries in relationships are just as necessary and beneficial as boundaries in the physical world.

**"And God said, 'Let there be light,'
and there was light.
God saw that the light was good,
and he separated the light
from the darkness."
(Genesis 1:3–4)**

Five Biblical Truths about Boundaries

Misconceptions about boundaries abound, but God's Word reveals these fundamental truths:

1. **Loving others requires boundaries.**

   God's Word reveals you cannot truly love a person without establishing limits.

   - Love is doing what is best for someone, which requires setting boundaries to identify and separate what is best and what is less than best.
   - Love is not being boundaryless nor is it two people morphing into one. Rather, it is the joining together of two different and distinct personalities in spiritual unity.

   The love you have for others is to mirror the love that Jesus declares for you.

   "As the Father has loved me, so have I loved you" (John 15:9).

2. **Obeying God demands boundaries.**

   Jesus did not do what everyone asked of Him, nor was He always available to everyone.

   - He said *no* to everyone and everything His Father said *no* to, and He said *yes* to everyone and everything His Father said *yes* to.
   - He wasn't depending on others to meet His needs for love, significance, or security, or to determine His purpose, but He was dependent on His Father.

When you take the position Jesus took and maintain that perspective, you will be free and empowered. Guilt and fear prevent intimacy, while boundaries protect confidence, love, and sound thinking.

"There is no fear in love. But perfect love drives out fear, because fear has to do with punishment. The one who fears is not made perfect in love" (1 John 4:18).

3. **Serving others necessitates boundaries.**

Not everyone will encourage you in developing Christlike character. Choose wisely with whom you will share yourself and your resources.

- Set limits on your use of time, love, energy, and finances, looking to God to help determine priorities for you and your resources.
- Identify the true need of others, discerning whether God intends for you to meet that need or for them to meet the need themselves.

Saying *no* may initially produce resentment, but with mutual respect and trust, in time the validity and necessity of your boundary will be understood.

"Carry each other's burdens, and in this way you will fulfill the law of Christ. . . . For each one should carry their own load" (Galatians 6:2, 5).

4. **Submission depends on boundaries.**

Boundaries and submission are equally necessary to be effective. Jesus submitted Himself to the will of His Father. Follow Christ's example, and submit to the boundaries He has laid out for your life and the purpose for which you were created.

- Biblical submission in relationships must be mutual—voluntary compliance is good for the other person and benefits the relationship.
- Biblical submission glorifies God, not a person. The result is humility rather than power or pride.

Scripture encourages you to submit to those the Lord has placed in your life to minister to you.

"The household of Stephanas . . . devoted themselves to the service of the Lord's people. I urge you . . . submit to such people and to everyone who joins in the work and labors at it" (1 Corinthians 16:15–16).

5. Selfishness cannot survive boundaries.

Godly boundaries are based on love and are not self-seeking. Boundaries are intended to protect God's children and ensure that His purposes are accomplished.

- Godly boundaries are an expression of selflessness, often requiring personal sacrifice and effort to both establish and maintain.
- Godly boundaries are often risky, evoking negative reactions from those who resent having limits or who do not want to take responsibility for their inappropriate behavior.

God's Word speaks to the wisdom of putting pride and selfishness aside.

"Follow God's example, therefore, as dearly loved children and walk in the way of love, just as Christ loved us and gave himself up for us as a fragrant offering and sacrifice to God" (Ephesians 5:1–2).

WHAT IS the Root Cause of Bad Boundaries?

God is love, and He made us for loving relationships. His love is the basis for our boundaries and is the glue that holds our relationships together.

When you love others, bond with them, express your own *boundaries*, and help them to achieve *healthy* boundaries as well, you exhibit God's love in action.

The Bible abounds with Scriptures about love because *"God is love."*

"And so we know and rely on the love God has for us. God is love. Whoever lives in love lives in God, and God in them. . . . Dear friends, let us love one another, for love comes from God. Everyone who loves has been born of God and knows God. Whoever does not love does not know God, because God is love."
(1 John 4:16, 7–8)

Three God-Given Inner Needs

In reality, we have all been created with three God-given inner needs: the needs for love, significance, and security.[7]

▶ **Love**—to know that someone is unconditionally committed to our best interest

"My command is this: Love each other as I have loved you" (John 15:12).

- **Significance**—to know that our lives have meaning and purpose

  "I cry out to God Most High, to God who fulfills his purpose for me" (Psalm 57:2 ESV).

- **Security**—to feel accepted and a sense of belonging

  "Whoever fears the Lord has a secure fortress, and for their children it will be a refuge" (Proverbs 14:26).

The Ultimate Need-Meeter

Why did God give us these deep inner needs, knowing that people and self-effort fail us?

God gave us these inner needs so that we would come to know Him as our Need-Meeter. Our needs are designed by God to draw us into a deeper dependence on Christ. God did not create any person or position or any amount of power or possessions to meet the deepest needs in our lives.

If a person or thing *could* meet all our needs, we wouldn't need God! The Lord will use circumstances and bring positive people into our lives as an extension of His care and compassion, but ultimately only God can satisfy all the needs of our hearts.

**"The Lord will guide you always;
he will satisfy your needs
in a sun-scorched land
and will strengthen your frame.
You will be like a well-watered garden,
like a spring whose waters never fail."
(Isaiah 58:11)**

The apostle Paul revealed this truth by first asking, *"What a wretched man I am! Who will rescue me from this body that is subject to death?"* He then answers his own question by saying he is saved by *"Jesus Christ our Lord!"* (Romans 7:24–25).

All along, the Lord planned to meet our deepest needs for . . .

▶ **Love**

"I [the Lord] have loved you with an everlasting love; I have drawn you with unfailing kindness" (Jeremiah 31:3).

▶ **Significance**

"'For I know the plans I have for you,' declares the Lord, 'plans to prosper you and not to harm you, plans to give you hope and a future'" (Jeremiah 29:11).

▶ **Security**

"The Lord himself goes before you and will be with you; he will never leave you nor forsake you. Do not be afraid; do not be discouraged" (Deuteronomy 31:8).

The truth is that our God-given needs for love, significance, and security can be legitimately met in Christ Jesus!

Philippians 4:19 makes it plain . . .

"My God will meet all your needs according to the riches of his glory in Christ Jesus."

Since actions are based on beliefs, boundaries reflect what we believe. If our beliefs are wrong, our subsequent thoughts and behaviors will be wrong, and our boundaries will also be wrong. In other words, bad boundaries result from faulty thoughts that come from wrong beliefs. It is always wise to give thought to the basis for your boundaries because what you think in your heart reveals what sort of person you are.

"For as he thinks in his heart, so is he."
(Proverbs 23:7 NKJV)

▶ Wrong Belief

"If I set boundaries, I'll push people away and never get the love and approval I need to feel good about myself. I just want to feel accepted and secure in my relationships."[8]

▶ Right Belief

"I need to set beneficial boundaries and not live for the approval of others. This will help me establish healthy relationships. Because of my secure relationship with Christ, I know I am unconditionally loved and accepted."[9]

"This is love: not that we loved God, but that he loved us."
(1 John 4:10)

Entering into a personal relationship with God is both *inclusive* and *exclusive.*

It is *inclusive* because anybody can come. All are welcome to enter into a relationship with God in which He is our heavenly Father and we are His children. No race, gender, age barriers—no socioeconomic divides keep us from becoming a child of the Most High God.

But the way to God is also *exclusive.* Don't be deceived into thinking there are many paths to heaven or that all religions lead to an everlasting relationship with the Almighty. God Himself has set this boundary: The only way to a personal relationship with God and the only way to receive the free gift of eternal life is through only one person, *Jesus*, God the Son. Acts 4:12 is explicitly clear: *"Salvation is found in no one else, for there is no other name under heaven given to mankind by which we must be saved."*

"Believe in the Lord Jesus, and you will be saved" (Acts 16:31)

Four Points of God's Plan

1. God's Purpose for You is *Salvation.*

What was God's motivation in sending Jesus Christ to earth?

To express His love for you by saving you!

The Bible says, *"God so loved the world that he gave his one and only Son, that whoever believes in him shall not perish but have eternal life. For God did not send his Son into the world to condemn the world, but to save the world through him*" (John 3:16–17).

What was Jesus' purpose in coming to earth?

To forgive your sins, to empower you to have victory over sin, and to enable you to live a fulfilled life!

Jesus said, "*I have come that they may have life, and that they may have it more abundantly*" (John 10:10 NKJV).

2. Your Problem is *Sin*.

What exactly is sin?

Sin is living independently of God's standard—knowing what is right, but choosing what is wrong.

The Bible says, "*If anyone, then, knows the good they ought to do and doesn't do it, it is sin for them*" (James 4:17).

What is the major consequence of sin?

Spiritual death, eternal separation from God.

Scripture states, "*Your iniquities [sins] have separated you from your God*" (Isaiah 59:2).

"*The wages of sin is death, but the gift of God is eternal life in Christ Jesus our Lord*" (Romans 6:23).

3. God's Provision for You is the *Savior*.

Can anything remove the penalty for sin?

Yes! Jesus died on the cross to personally pay the penalty for your sins.

The Bible says, "*God demonstrates his own love for us in this: While we were still sinners, Christ died for us*" (Romans 5:8).

What is the solution to being separated from God?

Belief in (entrusting your life to) Jesus Christ as the only way to God the Father.

Jesus says, *"I am the way and the truth and the life. No one comes to the Father except through me"* (John 14:6).

"Believe in the Lord Jesus, and you will be saved" (Acts 16:31).

4. **Your Part is *Surrender*.**

   Give Christ control of your life, entrusting yourself to Him.

   "Jesus said to his disciples, 'Whoever wants to be my disciple must deny themselves and take up their cross [die to your own self-rule] and follow me. For whoever wants to save their life will lose it, but whoever loses their life for me will find it. What good will it be for someone to gain the whole world, yet forfeit their soul?' " (Matthew 16:24–26).

   Place your faith in (rely on) Jesus Christ as your personal Lord and Savior and reject your "good works" as a means of earning God's approval.

   "It is by grace you have been saved, through faith—and this is not from yourselves, it is the gift of God—not by works, so that no one can boast" (Ephesians 2:8–9).

The moment you choose to receive Jesus as your Lord and Savior—entrusting your life to Him—He comes to live inside you. Then He gives you His power to live the fulfilled life God has planned for you.

If you want to be fully forgiven by God and become the person God created you to be, you can tell Him in a simple, heartfelt prayer like this:

PRAYER OF SALVATION

"God, I want a real relationship with You.
I admit that many times
I've chosen to go my own way
instead of Your way.
Please forgive me for my sins.
Jesus, thank You for dying on the cross
to pay the penalty for my sins.
Come into my life to be my Lord
and my Savior.
Change me from the inside out
and make me the person
You created me to be.
In Your holy name I pray. Amen."

What Can You Now Expect?

If you sincerely prayed this prayer, look at what God says about you!

"If the Son sets you free,
you will be free indeed."
(John 8:36)

STEPS TO SOLUTION

It's New Year's Day, and Allison finds herself in a bizarre, bone-chilling environment. But this has nothing to do with the weather.

Standing in her grown son's home, she's stunned by the scene around her. Imagine: the contents of cabinets and drawers are strewn throughout the house, the pungent odor of alcohol bottles, and the charred smell of cigarette butts smothers her senses—and altogether it's breaking her heart. Sprayed shards of broken glass crackle underfoot from a smoke bomb, making the trek from one room to the next ever more treacherous.

Everywhere Allison walks, she encounters trash and *filth*. She also discovers a glass aquarium housing two large boa constrictors, adding yet another dimension to the unsettling scene before her.

A dark, ominous sensation washes over Allison, and she finds herself reciting:[10]

"Even though I walk through
the darkest valley,
I will fear no evil, for you are with me;
your rod and your staff,
they comfort me."
(Psalm 23:4)

Key Verse to Memorize

2 Timothy 1:7

As Allison sifts through the contents of her son's house of horrors, she is sadly mindful of her encounter when arriving. A SWAT team officer informs her that a team has swept through the premises and provided the following report: "The bust was good. Clean. He's going to have a hard time getting out of this one."[11] He is Allison's only child, both rebel and prodigal. He's not a tumultuous teenager, but an adult who never learned boundaries.

Allison can't imagine finding any more surprises in the squalor before her. Surely nothing more can shock her senses. At least that's what she thinks. But Allison draws on the strength of the Spirit when she sees what is displayed in a lighted cabinet in the living room.[12]

Gratefully, God's Word assures . . .

"For the Spirit God gave us
does not make us timid,
but gives us power,
love and self-discipline."
(2 Timothy 1:7)

Key Passage to Read

Romans 13:1–14

Is it? No, it *can't* be! Looking closer, Allison discovers an entire collection of Nazi memorabilia on display—a large swastika, arm bands, flags, helmets, belt buckles, and photos—all commemorating the most twisted and vile form of collective corruption. During its reign of terror, the Third Reich flagrantly violated all of God's commandments, seeking instead to establish its own dark kingdom with its own rules—all based on hate.

Allison's spirit is wounded. How could her son, her only child, who once professed faith in Jesus Christ, cross into such evil territory?[13] Allison's anger is a legitimate response to her son's folly, for the Bible gives this specific instruction . . .

"Do not give the devil a foothold."
(Ephesians 4:27)

Boundaries in Life

Boundaries are critical safeguards designed by God to govern every area of life. This principle is clearly expressed in the New Testament. When God established the church, He clearly defined relational boundaries for all who would place their faith in Jesus as Lord and Savior.

Obey the Governing Authorities

"(1) Let everyone be subject to the governing authorities, for there is no authority except that which God has established. The authorities that exist have been established by God. . . . (5) Therefore, it is necessary to submit to the authorities, not only because of possible punishment but also as a matter of conscience. (6) This is also why you pay taxes, for the authorities are God's servants, who give their full time to governing. (7) Give

to everyone what you owe them: If you owe taxes, pay taxes; if revenue, then revenue; if respect, then respect; if honor, then honor" (Romans 13:1, 5–7).

- ▶ **We** are to be subject to all civil authorities because they are allowed by God. (v. 1)
- ▶ **We** are to submit to the authorities to avoid punishment and to have a clear conscience. (v. 5)
- ▶ **We** are to pay taxes to the authorities because they are full-time servants of God. (v. 6)
- ▶ **We** are to give to others what we owe them, be it taxes, revenue, respect, or honor. (v. 7)

Fulfill the Law through Love

"(8) Let no debt remain outstanding, except the continuing debt to love one another, for whoever loves others has fulfilled the law. (9) The commandments, 'You shall not commit adultery,' 'You shall not murder,' 'You shall not steal,' 'You shall not covet,' and whatever other command there may be, are summed up in this one command: 'Love your neighbor as yourself.' (10) Love does no harm to a neighbor. Therefore love is the fulfillment of the law" (Romans 13:8–10).

- ▶ **We** are to love others, leaving no debt except our continuing obligation to love everyone. (v. 8)
- ▶ **We** are to love people always because love meets every requirement of God. (v. 8)
- ▶ **We** are to love others because all of God's commandments are based on love. (v. 9)
- ▶ **We** are to love others because love harms no one, and thus it fulfills the whole law of God. (v. 10)

Put on the Lord Christ Jesus

"(11) And do this, understanding the present time: The hour has already come for you to wake up from your slumber, because our salvation is nearer now than when we first believed. (12) The night is nearly over; the day is almost here. So let us put aside the deeds of darkness and put on the armor of light. (13) Let us behave decently, as in the daytime, not in carousing and drunkenness, not in sexual immorality and debauchery, not in dissension and jealousy. (14) Rather, clothe yourselves with the Lord Jesus Christ, and do not think about how to gratify the desires of the flesh" (Romans 13:11–14).

- ▶ **We** are to love with a sense of urgency, keeping in mind that Christ's return is near. (v. 11)
- ▶ **We** are to reject sinful ways and let Christ live through us since His coming is so near. (v. 12)
- ▶ **We** are to behave as though Christ is here, not as though sin still reigns over us. (v. 13)
- ▶ **We** are to submit to Christ's rule over our lives rather than to sinful desires. (v. 14)

HOW TO Have a Transformed Life

After surveying the damage and the demented possessions of her prodigal, Allison Bottke makes a sobering observation: "Everywhere I looked was evidence of a life lived not on the edge, but somewhere deeper—in a pathetic pit of depravity. The tumor of [alcohol and drug] addiction, irresponsibility, recklessness, and crime could not be excised. It kept returning, each time more lethal than the last. The stench of a wasted life filled my nostrils."[14]

What her son, Christopher, *desperately* needs and Allison *desperately* acknowledges, is a transformed life.

The Bible clearly warns . . .

> **"The prudent see danger and take refuge, but the simple keep going and pay the penalty."**
> **(Proverbs 27:12)**

Reaching the Target: Transformation!

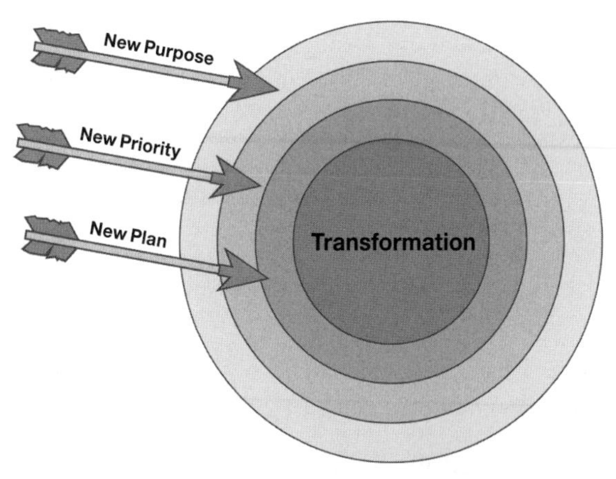

The Freedom Formula

	A New Purpose
+	**A New Priority**
+	**A New Plan**
	A Transformed Life

Target 1—A New Purpose: God's purpose for me is to be conformed to the character of Christ.

> *"Those God foreknew he also predestined to be conformed to the image of his Son"* (Romans 8:29).

- "I'll do whatever it takes to be conformed to the character of Christ."

Target 2—A New Priority: God's priority for me is to change my thinking.

> *"Do not conform to the pattern of this world, but be transformed by the renewing of your mind"* (Romans 12:2).

- "I'll do whatever it takes to line up my thinking with God's thinking."

Target 3—A New Plan: God's plan for me is to rely on Christ's strength, not my strength, to be all He created me to be.

> *"I can do all things through Christ who strengthens me"* (Philippians 4:13 NKJV).

- "I'll do whatever it takes to fulfill His plan in His strength."

My Personalized Plan To Be a Boundary Builder

I'm setting my sights on living the transformed life God desires for me and has made available through the life of Jesus Christ within me. I will look to boundaries as a tool to help me become more Christlike in my relationships and more effective in building boundaries.

I will . . .

BUILD healthy boundaries

- God loves me and wants me to establish healthy boundaries.
- It's never too late to begin learning how to set new boundaries.
- Change will be difficult, but the Lord will guide me and be my strength.

"The LORD is my strength and my shield; my heart trusts in him, and he helps me" (Psalm 28:7).

OVERCOME the fear of others' disapproval of my boundaries

- Personalize and memorize:

  "Am I now trying to win the approval of human beings, or of God? Or am I trying to please people? If I were still trying to please people, I would not be a servant of Christ" (Galatians 1:10).

- Personalize and memorize:

  "Be strong and courageous. Do not be afraid or terrified because of them, for the Lord your God goes with you; he will never leave you nor forsake you" (Deuteronomy 31:6).

- Personalize and memorize:

  "We speak as those approved by God to be entrusted with the gospel. We are not trying to please people but God, who tests our hearts" (1 Thessalonians 2:4).

UNDERSTAND that boundaries are biblical

- God established boundaries from the very beginning.
- God has His own personal boundaries.
- God expects me to live my life according to the boundaries He has laid out for me in Scripture.

"I am the LORD your God; consecrate yourselves and be holy, because I am holy" (Leviticus 11:44).

NOTIFY others of my boundaries (family, friends, coworkers)

- Recognize my resources and responsibilities.
- Communicate my convictions clearly.
- Share with sympathy and compassion the reasons I am establishing healthier boundaries.

"Speaking the truth in love, we will grow to become in every respect the mature body of him who is the head, that is, Christ" (Ephesians 4:15).

DEVELOP relationships with people who have healthy boundaries

- Seek to be around people who have healthy boundaries
- Ask God to bring mature people into my life to befriend me and advise me
- Become more aware of boundary violations and then address them

"Walk with the wise and become wise, for a companion of fools suffers harm" (Proverbs 13:20).

ADMIT my limitations and keep on trying

- Identify people I need to forgive who have violated my boundaries
- Ask forgiveness of those whose boundaries I have violated
- Commit to start over each time I fail

"Bear with each other and forgive one another if any of you has a grievance against someone. Forgive as the Lord forgave you" (Colossians 3:13).

REALIZE the need to set and maintain new boundaries

- The bonding process beginning in infancy is the most powerful influence on boundary building. Even if it was inadequate, it doesn't mean I can't build healthy boundaries as an adult.
- Identify and evaluate the boundaries formed in childhood, and determine which ones may be counterproductive in my life now as an adult.
- Make a plan to replace the harmful boundaries formed in childhood with new, beneficial ones.

"Forget the former things; do not dwell on the past. See, I am doing a new thing! Now it springs up; do you not perceive it? I am making a way in the wilderness and streams in the wasteland" (Isaiah 43:18–19).

IDENTIFY healthy boundaries for myself and commit to maintaining them

- Regularly review and assess my boundaries

- State what I will do if others cross my boundaries
- Follow through when my boundaries are crossed

"My words come from an upright heart; my lips sincerely speak what I know" (Job 33:3).

ENCOURAGE my family members to establish boundaries

- Share my decision to establish healthy, beneficial boundaries
- Express my gratitude for their different but meaningful roles in my life
- Invite them to join with me as I seek to please God and be the person He created me to be

"May the God who gives endurance and encouragement give you the same attitude of mind toward each other that Christ Jesus had" (Romans 15:5).

SEE my identity in Christ

- God chose me.
- God adopted me.
- God redeemed me.

"He chose us in him before the creation of the world . . . In love he predestined us for adoption to sonship through Jesus Christ, in accordance with his pleasure and will . . . In him [Christ] we have redemption through his blood, the forgiveness of sins, in accordance with the riches of God's grace" (Ephesians 1:4–7).

Angry Reactions from Others

Question: "How should I handle angry reactions from others when I attempt to set boundaries?"

Answer: There are typically two different methods people use to get others to do what they want them to do or keep them from doing what they don't want them to do—such as setting boundaries. While they are referred to as games, there is nothing fun about these methods.

▶ The Guilt Game

- As you establish healthy boundaries, others may try to make you feel guilty. This is false guilt. Hold your ground, and set your boundaries anyway.
- By establishing boundaries, you may be accused of not loving others. This is false guilt. Explain that setting boundaries is loving, and set your boundaries anyway.
- If in building your boundaries, you begin to feel that others may not love you or if you begin to question your love for them, set your boundaries anyway and pray this Scripture . . .

"When I am afraid, I put my trust in you. In God, whose word I praise—in God I trust and am not afraid. What can mere mortals do to me?" (Psalm 56:3–4).

▶ The Blame Game

- As you begin to establish boundaries and take charge of your life, others may become angry at having to adjust to the new you. They may blame you for their poor behavior and try to force you to return to old ways of being manipulated and controlled through guilt. Clarify that their response to your boundaries is their choice . . . and maintain your boundaries.

- Having healthy boundaries means not manipulating others and not being manipulated by others. Choose to not be manipulated . . . and maintain your boundaries.
- Be diligent to remember: A mind focused on the will of God will produce actions pleasing to God. Keeping correct boundaries is pleasing to God . . . so maintain your boundaries.

"Do not conform to the pattern of this world, but be transformed by the renewing of your mind. Then you will be able to test and approve what God's will is—his good, pleasing and perfect will" (Romans 12:2).

Setting Good Boundaries

Question: "How do I begin the process of setting good boundaries?"

Answer: The best way to start the boundary-setting process is by reading God's Word and praying. These are two vital spiritual components for determining how to live a life that is both pleasing to God and fulfilling for you. You must lay a solid foundation, and that foundation is the Word of God.

Another important step is to follow the examples of people in your life who have firmly established, biblical boundaries. Seek their sound advice about where to start.

Be sure to . . .

Step 1: **Pray** for the Lord to clearly reveal your need and how to move forward.

Step 2: **Pinpoint** where your boundaries are weak and need to be reinforced.

Step 3: **Partner** with someone who will hold you accountable.

Step 4: **Prepare** to see changes in your relationships with others.

Step 5: **Permit** yourself to acknowledge successes internally. Boundary building is hard work!

Step 6: **Put together** a support system of friends and family for strength in the potential "danger zones" that can trigger old responses.

Step 7: **Prioritize** the people with whom you want to set boundaries and identify the situations in which you need to set limits. Don't try to tackle all of them at one time.

As you commit your plans and efforts to God and begin the process of working with your accountability partner, remember:

**"Two are better than one,
because they have a good return
for their labor."
(Ecclesiastes 4:9)**

Even though Christopher is an adult, Allison Bottke can no longer deny her part in the downward spiral that characterizes her son's life.

For too many years she has been both mother and *enabler,* nurturing and protecting to a fault. Allison recognizes that her overly safeguarding control has not only sheltered Christopher from painful consequences but also prevented him from learning valuable life lessons. Her maternal enabling has also contributed to Christopher's warped perception of reality, leading to excuses for allowing chaos to rule his life.

Sitting in a courtroom for her son's arraignment hearing concerning the New Year's Day debacle, Allison hears the charges read, a court date set, and bond announced at $10,000. Only 10% is needed to release Christopher from custody, so the bail bondsman assures Allison, "If you can pay the $1,000, we'll have him out of here in no time." Allison responds: "No."

"No?" he inquires.

Allison affirms: "That's correct."[15]

The parental boundary stuns the bail bondsman and prompts Christopher to scowl. It's been a long time coming, but Allison is determined to begin building healthy boundaries.[16]

The Bible provides direction for parents like Allison:

> **"If any of you lacks wisdom,**
> **you should ask God,**
> **who gives generously**
> **to all without finding fault,**
> **and it will be given to you."**
> **(James 1:5)**

Six Sure Steps for Success

You need a plan, as well as a counselor, mentor, pastor, or friend who will walk alongside you as you rely on God to help you gain control of your life. As you continually face the challenges required to maintain healthy boundaries, remember that . . .

> **"Those who hope in the Lord**
> **will renew their strength.**
> **They will soar on wings like eagles;**
> **they will run and not grow weary,**
> **they will walk and not be faint."**
> **(Isaiah 40:31)**

1. Admit you have a problem.

Acknowledge you're the one who lacks boundaries, and turn to God for help and insight.

"Search me, God, and know my heart; test me and know my anxious thoughts. See if there is any offensive way in me, and lead me in the way everlasting" (Psalm 139:23–24).

2. **Be aware you may have times when you will not want to do the hard work of change.**

   Admit you've often been your own worst enemy, even though you have placed blame elsewhere.

   "Yet you desired faithfulness even in the womb; you taught me wisdom in that secret place" (Psalm 51:6).

3. **Care about yourself enough to prioritize God's work in your life.**

   Determine to leave others in His care. Agree to let God change you.

   "Therefore, with minds that are alert and fully sober, set your hope on the grace to be brought to you when Jesus Christ is revealed at his coming" (1 Peter 1:13).

4. **Don't try to set all new boundaries at the same time.**

   Make small changes before you take on bigger challenges.

   "Consider it pure joy, my brothers and sisters, whenever you face trials of many kinds, because you know that the testing of your faith produces perseverance. Let perseverance finish its work so that you may be mature and complete, not lacking anything" (James 1:2–4).

5. **Enforce boundaries consistently in your quest to become more Christlike, even when you don't feel like it.**

   Accept the challenge to enforce boundaries.

   "Physical training is good, but training for godliness is much better, promising benefits in this life and in the life to come" (1 Timothy 4:8 NLT).

6. **CONTINUE to move forward, and resist urges to fall back into old unhealthy patterns.**

   Grieve the losses that naturally occur with change as you seek to fulfill your God-given purpose.

   "Blessed is the one who perseveres under trial because, having stood the test, that person will receive the crown of life that the Lord has promised to those who love him" (James 1:12).

HOW TO Communicate Boundary Changes

After Allison confirms she won't bail Christopher out of jail, he scrounges together the funds to free himself temporarily. Shortly thereafter, he makes his displeasure known through painful words that pierce his mother's heart like a knife.

Christopher has seen his mother's tears in the courtroom, and he caustically summarizes the scene: "You put on quite a show in the courtroom . . . you cried so everyone would feel sorry for you."[17]

The inconceivable coldness of his cruel accusation motivates Allison to maintain boundaries that will help heal her wounded heart and hopefully transform Christopher's hardened heart.

Christopher's callousness reveals this sad reality of rebellion . . .

> **"For everyone looks out for their own interests, not those of Jesus Christ." (Philippians 2:21)**

Life is made up of different seasons that sometimes require transitional conversations to ease the discomfort often created by change. When grown children leave home and especially when they get married, they enter a new season of life that not only impacts them but their parents as well.

During these times, relationships change and may need to be redefined. Having loving conversations regarding boundary changes can be helpful and meaningful, encouraging growth and solidifying relationships.

If you realize that you have not made a healthy transition from your family of origin to your new family, you may need to set and communicate new boundaries.

Communicating Boundaries

In Marriage

Marriage is a covenant commitment between one man and one woman *"and the two will become one flesh"* (Mark 10:8). Boundaries are about defining your respective selves in the midst of this God-ordained union.

Marriage can become fertile ground for boundary issues to sprout and grow if not properly addressed. A healthy marriage consists of two complete people who together create an environment of love. They do not need each other to be complete, but they share a loving union that God compares to our relationship with Christ.

▶ **State** what you need.

"I love you and love our time together, but I also need time to be by myself."

▶ **Establish** boundaries that explain how you expect to be treated.

"I love you and want our marriage to work, but if you choose to treat me in this way, there will be repercussions. If you ________, I will ________."

▶ **Define** what acceptable communication means to you:

"I will not be talked to in a hateful way, especially not in front of the children. If you choose to speak to me disrespectfully, I will ask you to leave our home until you can speak in a kind voice. If you refuse, then I will remove myself temporarily from your presence."

> **"Do not let any unwholesome talk**
> **come out of your mouths,**
> **but only what is helpful**
> **for building others up**
> **according to their needs,**
> **that it may benefit those who listen."**
> **(Ephesians 4:29)**

In Friendships

▶ **Define** your relationship.

"I'm glad we have so much in common, such as our love of biking and exploring new places."

▶ **Establish** and maintain boundaries.

"It's great that we can get together every other week for our outings. Let's meet at my house Saturday after next and have breakfast together before starting our morning adventure."

- **Reinforce** limitations.

  "I'm sorry you can't meet this week, but Saturday is the only time I have available."

"The righteous choose their friends carefully, but the way of the wicked leads them astray."
(Proverbs 12:26)

In Parenting

- **Establish** limits.

  "Please use your *inside voice* when you play in our home and your *outside voice* when you play in the yard."

- **Define** repercussions.

  "If you choose to __________, the repercussion is ________."

- **Explain** appropriate behavior.

  "In our home we do not hit each other. Because each of us is a gift from God, we love one another."

"Children are a gift from the Lord."
(Psalm 127:3 NLT)

In the Workplace

- **Stay** within the scope of your job description.

  "I was hired to do a specific job. I am now being asked to do things that are not a part of that original agreement. I understand occasional extra assignments will arise, but this extra time is becoming the 'norm' and not the exception. I feel I have been asked to take on more responsibilities than I was hired to perform. Can we talk about my job description, expectations, and level of compensation?"

- **Define** your work parameters.

  "I need to complete many time-sensitive tasks, and it's important that I finish my work while I'm here. I am happy to schedule a time to discuss collaborative projects. Thank you for respecting my time and working together as a team."

- **Work** within the boundaries of your schedule.

  "Please know how grateful I am for all that I have learned since I've been here and for the opportunity to contribute to (_name_). I need to discuss an important issue with you. (_State request._) I was hired to work 'X' number of hours each week. I understand there will be occasional emergencies or deadlines, and I want to be a team player. But four out of the last six weeks I've worked overtime. My work is important to me, but so is my family. How can we work together to achieve a healthy work/family balance?"

"Now to the one who works, wages are not credited as a gift but as an obligation" (Romans 4:4).

HOW TO Respond When Boundaries Are Crossed

Despite Allison Bottke's resolve to love her son without taking responsibility from him, a litany of excuses threatens to destabilize the boundaries she establishes for Christopher. She is forced to prepare a firm response for attempted infractions.

Concerning the turmoil still characterizing Christopher's life, Allison lends a listening ear rather than extending a helping hand. She no longer rushes to rescue Christopher from every crisis to protect him from pain. Pain is precisely how God achieves some of His best work—His transforming work.[33]

Scripture promises:

"The fruit of that righteousness will be peace; its effect will be quietness and confidence forever."
(Isaiah 32:17)

We all have physical, moral, and personal boundaries that should not be violated. Do you know your specific boundaries? Do you know how to respond when your boundary limits have been trampled? Do you know where to draw the line? The following responses will help you alert those in your life who verbally and emotionally cross the line. Do not let fear keep you from enforcing your boundaries.

"Fear of man will prove to be a snare, but whoever trusts in the Lord is kept safe."
(Proverbs 29:25)

- ▶ **Inform**: "Do you realize that you are speaking loudly?"

  "Do you know you are saying things that are making me feel uncomfortable?"

- ▶ **Identify**: "Please don't use that kind of language."

  "Please explain your anger."

- ▶ **Implore**: "Stop insulting me with your words."

  "Stop hurting me in this way."

- ▶ **Insist**: "You may not continue to hurt me this way."

  "You will have to change your way of communicating with me."

- ▶ **Instruct:** "When you talk with me, this is what I will expect ..."

  "When you (name behavior), it deeply hurts me. This is what I want you to do ... "

- ▶ **Invite**: "I care about you and our relationship, but the way you communicate with me needs to change."

  "I'm willing to go to counseling together, if you are in agreement."

- ▶ **Impact**: "This behavior has become unacceptable to me, so I'm distancing myself from you for a time."

  "I will be away for (hours) to give each of us space/time to cool down and give some thought to our problem. I will be back to resolve this conflict peacefully and respectfully at that time."

Although verbal boundaries are difficult to establish and may appear wounding to someone who is emotionally upset and unwilling to assume responsibility for hurtful actions, they are necessary for healing. These words from King Solomon emphasize this reality . . .

"Wounds from a friend can be trusted, but an enemy multiplies kisses." (Proverbs 27:6).

HOW TO Maintain Your Boundaries

The flow of money and material things from Allison's hand to Christopher's has stopped. Instead, Allison Bottke maintains a disciplined choice to teach Christopher responsibility, while at the same time protecting her heart from continual pain.

Christopher repeatedly tells his mom everything will be "okay," but she wants much more for him than "okay."[18] Allison knows boundaries will help Christopher build a better life. Ultimately, the answers for Christopher will come from his relationship with God and his dependence on Him, not his mother. Allison knows she must stop being an obstacle to her son's need for the Lord, and she acknowledges this truth: "I've often said this: When I stopped trying to be God in my son's life, he found God."[19]

Scripture teaches . . .

"Whoever scorns instruction will pay for it, but whoever respects a command is rewarded." (Proverbs 13:13)

Maintaining Boundaries

After you establish boundaries, it is common for those around you to test them to see whether you really intend to maintain them. These people have been accustomed to getting what they want, so they try to get you to revert back to your past behavior.

Remember this counsel from God's Word . . .

**"If you do what is right,
will you not be accepted?
But if you do not do what is right,
sin is crouching at your door;
it desires to have you,
but you must rule over it."
(Genesis 4:7)**

► **Pay attention** to your feelings and watch for warning signs that you are beginning to lose sight of your boundaries.

- Remind yourself of why you set the boundary in the first place.
- Remember, repercussions are good. They exist because some people may try to overstep your boundaries.
- Rehearse what God's Word says.

"Be on your guard; stand firm in the faith; be courageous; be strong. Do everything in love" (1 Corinthians 16:13–14).

- **Plan ahead** by role-playing with a friend or even by yourself in front of a mirror on how to say *no.*
  - Begin with simple situations where saying *no* has less impact. For example, saying *no* to a telemarketer who calls: "I'm sorry, but I must say *no*. Goodbye." If the telemarketer is persistent, just say, "I really am not interested," and gently hang up the phone.
  - Be aware of how you feel after hanging up the phone. Thank God by reaffirming that the boundary was good for you.
  - Believe that as you continue to enforce your boundaries it will become easier to maintain them through self-control.

"The fruit of the Spirit is love, joy, peace, forbearance, kindness, goodness, faithfulness, gentleness and self-control. Against such things there is no law" (Galatians 5:22–23).

- **Recognize** that guilty feelings you may have over setting appropriate boundaries is false guilt. It is healthy for you to establish and maintain personal boundaries.
  - Appreciate the importance of consistency with your boundaries, helping others honor them by maintaining and enforcing them.
  - Apply the repercussion when your boundary has been violated.
  - Always keep the end goal in mind as you persevere.

"Whoever disregards discipline comes to poverty and shame, but whoever heeds correction is honored" (Proverbs 13:18).

▶ **Rejoice** as you continue to keep your personal boundaries, and delight in your newfound freedom.

- Trust that God will give you strength for this journey.
- Treasure the truth that boundaries are important to everyone and are not negative. Personal boundaries are set to protect, not to offend.
- Thank God that He has given you tremendous value by sacrificing His only Son for you. And as His child, you are worthy of protecting yourself with boundaries.

"Rejoice always . . . give thanks in all circumstances; for this is God's will for you in Christ Jesus" (1 Thessalonians 5:16, 18).

It's said that *good fences make good neighbors* by designating property lines and marking boundaries. A good fence is designed to keep out unwanted intrusions and form a protective shield for those inside. For a fence not to be a prison, a gate is required, allowing access and admittance when open, but continuing to shield and protect when closed.

Jesus says . . .

"I am the gate;
whoever enters through me will be saved.
They will come in and go out,
and find pasture."
(John 10:9)

Because the concept of boundaries began with God, the healthiest relationships have boundaries. They protect both your heart and your home.

—June Hunt

SCRIPTURES TO MEMORIZE

How can I know **what God's will is** for me?

> *"Do not conform to the pattern of this world, but be transformed by the renewing of your mind. Then you will be able to test and approve* ***what God's will is****—his good, pleasing and perfect will"* (Romans 12:2).

What **things** should I **think about** all the time, including when considering boundaries?

> *"Finally, brothers and sisters, whatever is true, whatever is noble, whatever is right, whatever is pure, whatever is lovely, whatever is admirable—if anything is excellent or praiseworthy—****think about*** *such* ***things****"* (Philippians 4:8).

How can I **stand firm** and be **set free** instead of being **burdened**?

> *"It is for freedom that Christ has* ***set*** *us* ***free****.* ***Stand firm****, then, and do not let yourselves be* ***burdened*** *again by a yoke of slavery"* (Galatians 5:1).

To whom must **each of us give an account of ourselves**?

> *"****Each of us*** *will* ***give an account of ourselves*** *to God"* (Romans 14:12).

Why should I **forget the past**?

> *"****Forget*** *the former things; do not dwell on* ***the past****. See, I am doing a new thing!"* (Isaiah 43:18–19).

Why shouldn't I **fear punishment**?

*"There is no fear in love. But perfect love drives out fear, because **fear** has to do with **punishment**. The one who fears is not made perfect in love"* (1 John 4:18).

Does the **Spirit God gave** me **make** me **timid** or give me **power, love, and self-discipline**?

*"For the **Spirit God gave** us does not **make** us **timid**, but gives us **power, love and self-discipline**"* (2 Timothy 1:7).

How can I **demolish arguments** and **take every thought captive**?

*"We **demolish arguments** and every pretension that sets itself up against the knowledge of God, and we **take captive every thought** to make it obedient to Christ"* (2 Corinthians 10:5).

Can I serve **Christ** if I am **trying to please people** and **win** their **approval**?

*"Am I now trying to **win** the **approval** of human beings, or of God? Or am I **trying to please people**? If I were still trying to please people, I would not be a servant of **Christ**"* (Galatians 1:10).

Since I have been **approved by God**, should I try to **please people** or **God**?

*"We speak as those **approved by God** to be entrusted with the gospel. We are not trying to **please people** but **God**, who tests our hearts"* (1 Thessalonians 2:4).